GO
CODA CANOR LUX

JACK QUIN

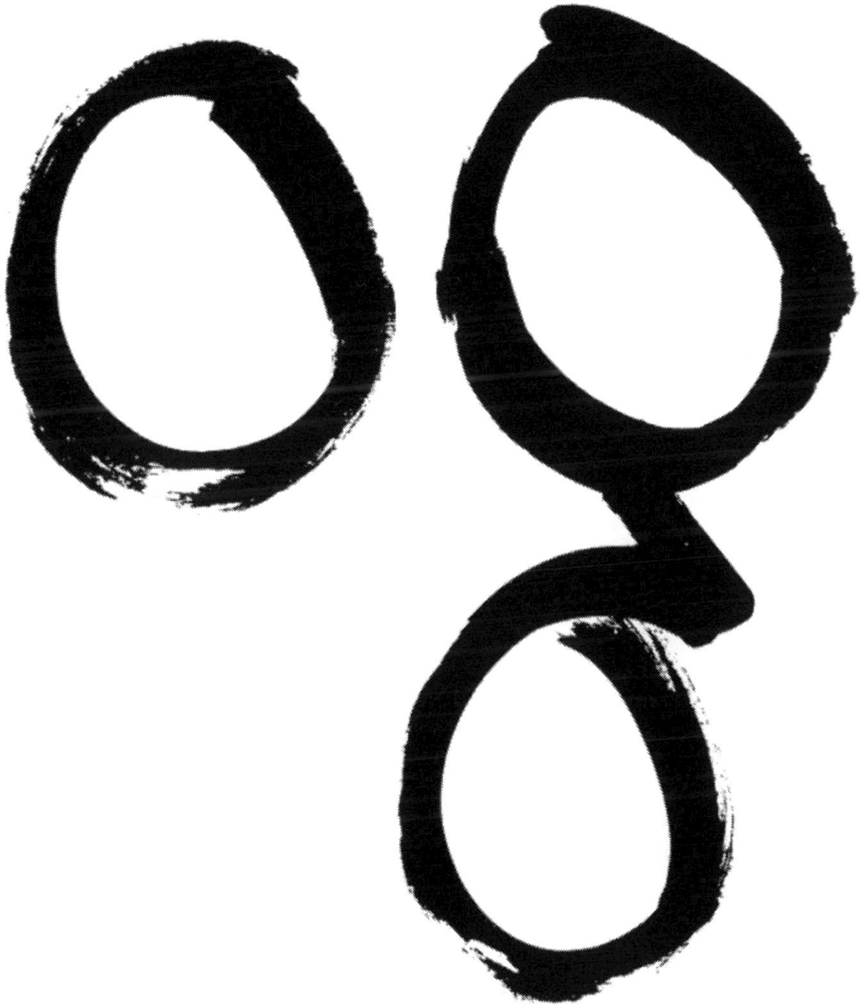

for Woo Jung and Amie
with thanks to family
and friends
near far and in between

Preface

Go is a word of wonder. Its usages include meaning to move, to say, to try, to happen, to divide and to act in harmony. Fundamentally, it's what everyone and everything is doing all the time.

Go has other meanings too. It's a programming language. It's a transit system. It's a square to pass.

Go is also the English name for the ancient Chinese game Weiqi. Renowned throughout the ages for the complex universes it creates, it is elegant simplicity in both rules and form. Fittingly, it is said to be a muse of both the Daodejing and Yijing.

Go is a sentence unto itself; it's why and how all of our stories begin.

Sincerely,

JQ

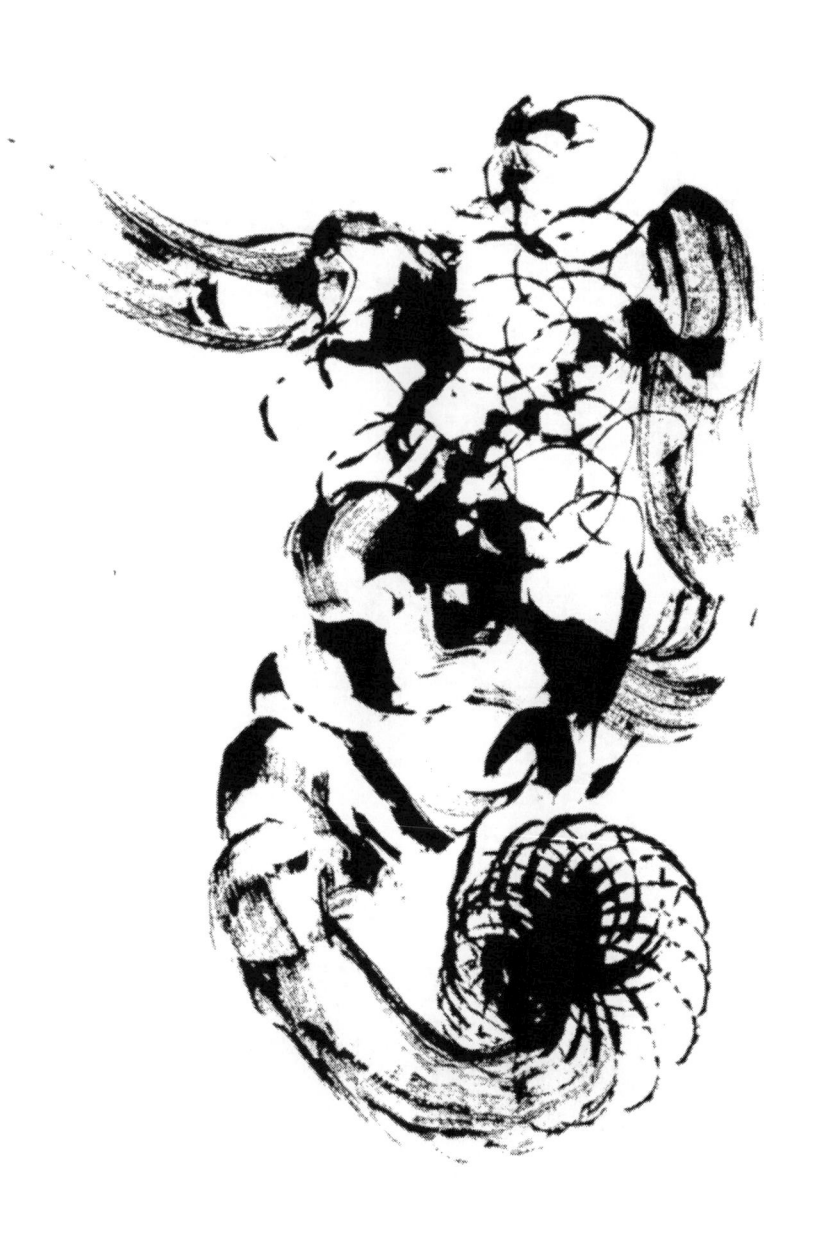

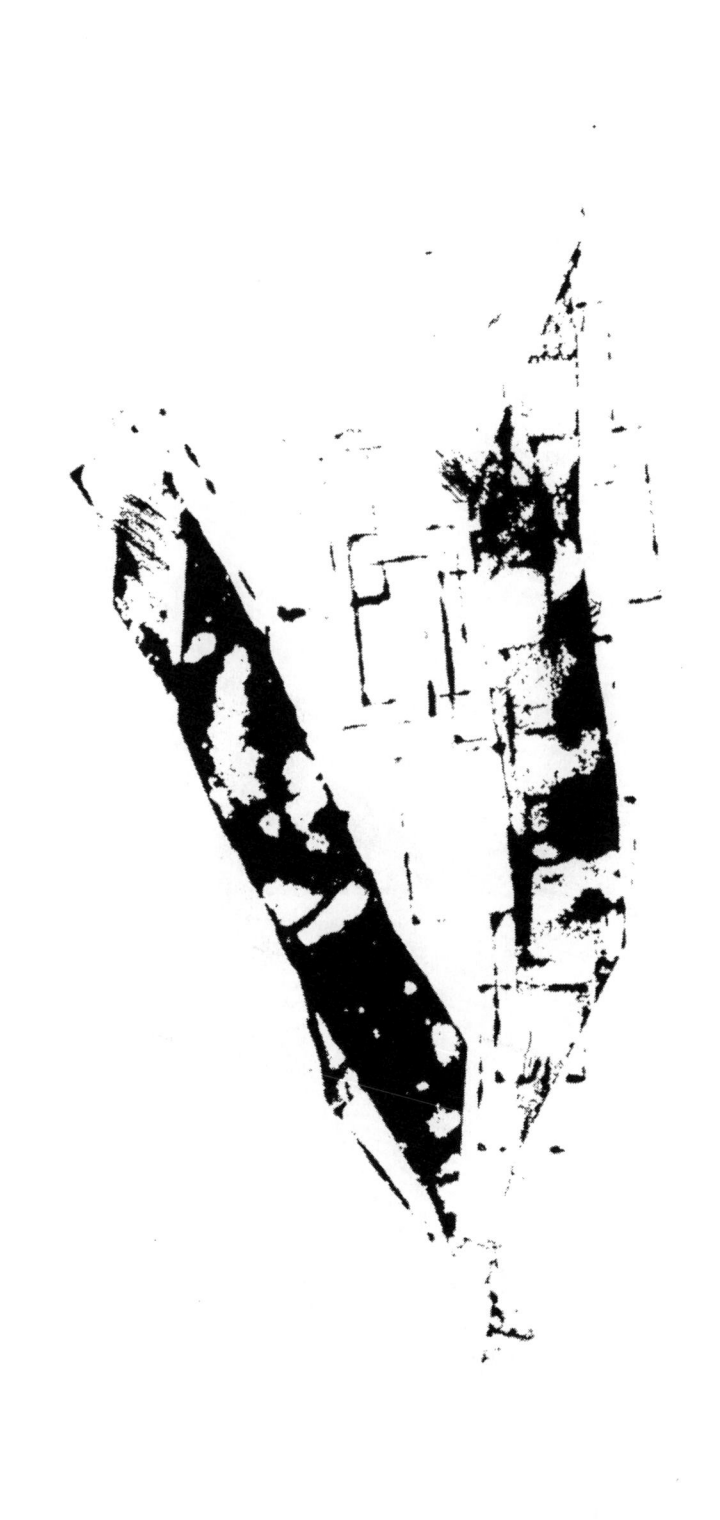

turtle was now always
turtle was egg
in the belly of mama universe

so much love
he grew
splashed out into
lush liquid light
swam all over
played among stars
all bright echoes and happy
until
the wonder

the wonder came with
the burning
and the burning said
look upon
and turtle looked

mama universe smiled and said
free

then turtle did

the coming down

he went

down

down

down

down

down

cast from stars

and so too his shell

and the coming down was hard

on turtle

and ho!
on the down
the wonder became
the wander
and for the first time
turtle walked
for the first time
saw other than light
heard other than echoes
for the first time
turtle spoke
turtle said
whoa!

wandering the down
turtled filled all up
got tired
so took to sleeping
right where he was at
knowing not knowing
not knowing knowing
right 'neath
moon

moon nigh

was dancing

round around round

'tween twirls

she saw turtle a'sleeping

all full alone on the down

no shell to hold him round

and so

sang to him

and moon's songs slipped
right into turtle
where they strummed
hummed
and pipped
till the last ash of twilight
was swept
till sun took
to rising

turtle woke
and through his heart
sun spoke
sun said
turtle go
turtle asked
a way can you show?
sun said
with the flow
and made way a'shining

turtle followed
lead belly slow

but on the down
and so low
turtle couldn't keep up and go
and soon got lost in
the reflection
the ever beginning
where about and all around
rippling every way is light
even where there isn't
and it's so bright
turtle closed his eyes
and went
deep in

turtle looked round the reflection
up sides
down sides
every way he was and already there
and turtle thought
for the first time
nowhere was there
for turtle to hide
and thinking that
forgot
most every all else

forgot starlight swimming
forgot happy splash play
forgot mama universe love
forgot echoes made
so in the reflection
turtle stayed

mama universe murmured
the see

when the high way was
of sun's shine spent
moon came round to see
where turtle was at
heavin' and heavy with songs she'd caught
moon swung whole low and gold
so turtle she chanced to knock
out of the reflection and into
the dreaming

and that was when
about and all around
moon's songs spilled
which is why and how the down is
with moon songs filled

all save her self light spent
moon melted into the firmament
and was gone

lo!

no moon soon

turtle from the dreaming woke and

for the first time

felt cold

and the changing was hard

on turtle

i am said he

mama universe whisper wept
in thee

now turtle didn't then right know
the way of his change
but somehow remembered
go
of sun's saying
and so he started to walk
and with one step of all four
got to rock

who? asked turtle
rock said rock
and together they spoke

rock said he waited the beautiful
what's the beautiful? asked turtle
the beautiful is
the beautiful said rock
oh! said turtle
you gotta go see the beautiful turtle
said rock
how? asked turtle
why? because you're turtle said rock
am i?
you are
where is the beautiful rock?
i don't know where the beautiful is
but i do know where the beautiful was at

and turtle listened
and rock told

so are you gonna go? asked rock
i don't know said turtle
oh!? said rock
but should i do i'll ask the beautiful
to get back to you said turtle
thanks allot said rock

then turtle turned
and set foot
and as he walked
all the down shook

see you around turtle said rock
so long

wind blew

turtle got to where rock said
the beautiful was at
and from a mound looked round
for the beautiful
to be found
and heard
holla
hullo
and turned

are you the beautiful? asked turtle
i'm tree said tree
i'm turtle said turtle
pleased to meet you said tree
and you said turtle
is the beautiful here tree?

the beautiful comes
the beautiful goes
the beautiful rises
falls and sows
spoke tree

so!? said turtle
so would you like to see
the beautiful turtle? asked tree
yes said he
up said she
and tree bowed
and why!?
turtle climbed

from tree
turtle saw sun
turtle saw rock
and further turtle saw
the reflection

do you see the beautiful turtle?
asked tree
i see sun rock and the reflection
said turtle
and beyond? asked tree
and turtle tried to see beyond
i don't see the beautiful tree said turtle
and he got down

so are you going to go? asked tree
i don't know said turtle
it's hard to know which way to go
said tree
why? asked turtle
because you're turtle turtle

and turtle got heavy
as again those words he heard
see you around tree said turtle
and tree bowed
farewell said she
and turtle
got gone

cloud gathered

far from tree
far from rock
far from the reflection
turtle walked
till he was upside down

and turtle saw sun
and sun bade
then came stars
and turtle almost remembered stars
and stars faded
and turtle saw

who are we? asked turtle

sky said wind
wind said cloud
cloud said sky
they spoke and together

i am turtle said turtle

how did you get here turtle? asked sky
sun rock tree said turtle
how now are you going? asked wind
i don't know said turtle
if you don't know why go? asked cloud
don't i know said turtle
which way are you going turtle? asked sky
away from the reflection said turtle
away from the reflection he says?
asked cloud
away from the reflection he says said wind
but the reflection is of the beautiful
said cloud
so which way goes away?
why any and all the ways with which
whatsoever turtle plays said sky

whoa! said cloud
that's what i was going to say said wind
and right then turtle wondered
who? what? where? when? why? and how?
ways were made and said

i was told of the beautiful
that comes and goes
rises falls and sows
a way to the beautiful
please would you show?

and sky twinkled
opened and said
turtle the beautiful
does not begin
does not end
with you
deepens
and
depends

and so for seven suns
turtle was told
some ways to hold on
some ways to let go
which are both ways of the becoming
cloud said

there are so many ways
that to turtle they gleamed
another way to go
in between
and for the first time turtle smiled
and said thanks

you are well come
said the friends three
and so we part ways
now go on
be

sunset

how turtle got through
that way in between
only he knows
but somehow along
that way
was made in his bones
and it quivered a quaver inside him
as he wandered alone on the down
thinking so

the beautiful is somehow now
to be found

then it happened
turtle got to the thought
to find the beautiful
he ought to get back
to that cold hard
changing spot

but that thought
is so fraught with naught
and won't let be
that in a taut thought knot
turtle got caught
got lost in the dark
that he did not see

mama universe hallooed
to the stars abound
go show the glow slow below
to turtle in the dark on the down

turtle woke
and as one stars spoke
stars said turtle hope
turtle said turtle broke
hope broke gotta grope
said stars
hope broke gotta grope
and together played ways
of turtle's dreaming

from where he was at
turtle looked upon the stars
all a'glisten so wondrous through sky
and even ever more ways beyond
when sudden while seeing
their shimmer skip dip blip
as they shone
for the first time
turtle heard
moon's songs

who sings? called turtle
moon said moon
i'm turtle said turtle
hallo turtle
i thought you were the beautiful moon
said turtle
are you seeking the beautiful turtle?
asked moon
i am in a way i suppose said turtle
what do you see? asked moon
i see i don't knows

and the stars unbound their burning
one by one then all
till slow the flow glowed over bursting
turtle even gleaned one fall

i don't see you moon
still i am here
where?
amongst echoes and tears
is that far?
yes and near

i want to see you
please show me a way
and i will come to you

i cannot show you a way here turtle
why not?
it's not mine
whose is it?
thine

far away rock rolled
tree shed loose leaves
cloud wisped and thinned
sky glimmered and cleaved
wind whirled round the down
sun simmered and soared

then was a hush
all the down stilled
from out one of turtle's eyes
a drop of lightning spilled

and all turtle's bones
swirled and swished
deep within
a moon song
hallow and bold
trilled a rippling pitch

what's this? cried turtle

this is a song of old
of colours
and of ways

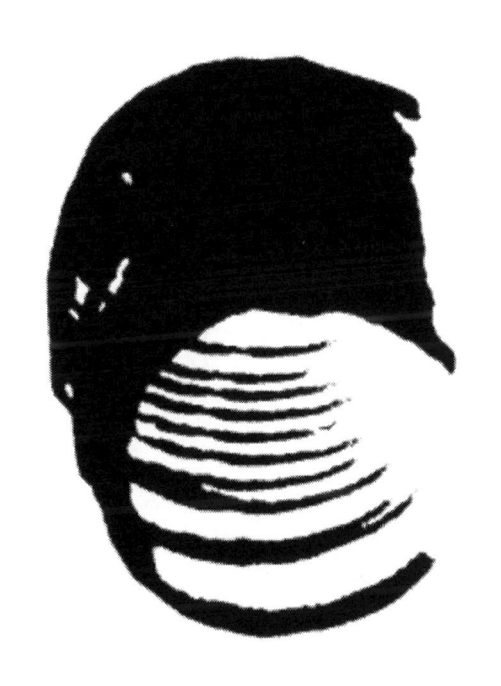

and right then
turtle cooed and bellowed
his first echo on the down he made

and ho!
throughout the down
that echo thundered
lit on turtle's lightning way
till turtle and too the wonder drummed

up slides
down strides
spoke turtle

and

gathered
all
in
aim

mama universe
blew moon to breath

free the see in thee
sang moon

and in the firmament
a ring of mist
with turtle's lightning mixed

turtle shivered
and crooned
a second echo
which cold cracked
the down
to bits

a third echo rambled and rose through sky
round around it went
till it stayed a'swaying
tucked tight round all the bits

a fourth echo shook and shot
from turtle's heart it came
and turtle went a'tumbling
through tears over bursting
and somehow wow!
a way

and then

a fifth echo rushed roared and rocked
and just as the first
lush liquid light hot
and it flowed over turtle
right where he was at

which is why and how
on the down is found wound

     wondrous

     amorous

     thrilling

     ethereal

     radiant

     sounds

and then
as the great waves weaved
for the first time
turtle knew peace
the song of colours and ways
was free

and lo!

turtle's mind

became

the colours and ways of stars

turtle's heart

the colours and ways of sun

turtle's spirit

the colours and ways of tree

turtle's eyes

the colours and ways of sky

turtle's breath

the colours and ways of wind

turtle's belly

the colours and ways of cloud

and turtle's back

the colours and ways of rock

and this is
who what where when why and how
a new shell was made for turtle
to wonder the down
and wander the see

so then
for the first time
upon the reflection
moon appeared
and turtle swam

beautifully

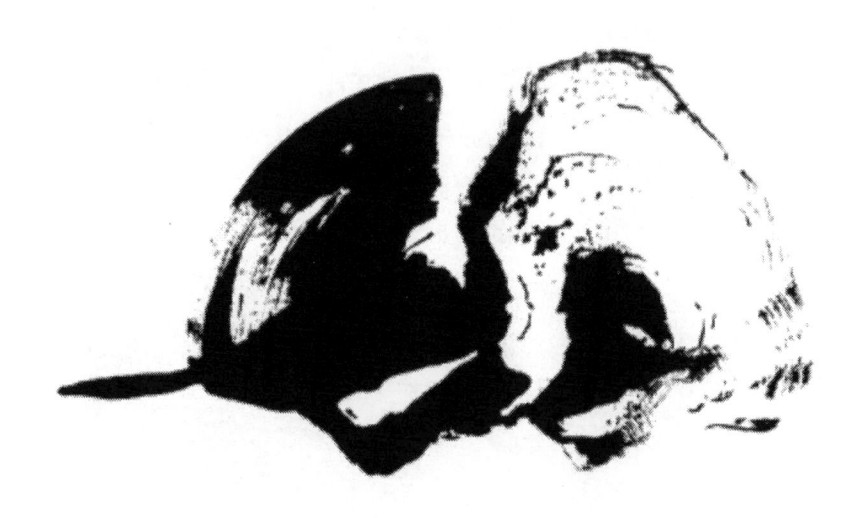

CODA CANOR LUX

the longing the ache the marrow quakes
the colour the shape the arrow awakes

lo' in ecstasy
sound and light are born entwined
and roam the void ride the deep tide

the distance the strength
great journey great length
through time through space the echoes race
all time all space destroy create
the beauty the grace great wonder a face

sound and light fill the void
in rapture sound is felled
light speeds on chaos swells

the longing the ache the arrow quakes
the colour the shape the marrow awakes

and in chaos a chorus resounds
echoes the love of light and sound
end of chaos a chorus resounds
echoes of love light and sound
eternally bound
eternally wound
eternally found

Made in the USA
Middletown, DE
26 June 2019